Fantastic Year 5 Punctuation practice from CGP!

The best way for pupils to improve their Punctuation in Year 5 (ages 9-10) is by doing as much practice as they can.

That's where this book comes in. It's packed with questions that'll test them on all the crucial Punctuation skills, including those introduced for the first time in Year 5.

And there's more! Everything is perfectly matched to the National Curriculum and we've included answers at the back. Enjoy!

What CGP is all about

Our sole aim here at CGP is to produce the highest quality books — carefully written, immaculately presented and dangerously close to being funny.

Then we work our socks off to get them out to you — at the cheapest possible prices.

Published by CGP
Editors
Keith Blackhall, Heather Cowley, Catherine Heygate, Gabrielle Richardson, Hayley Shaw, Sam Summers
With thanks to Andy Cashmore for the proofreading.

ISBN: 978 1 78294 125 5

Clipart from Corel®
Printed by Elanders Ltd, Newcastle upon Tyne.
Based on the classic CGP style created by Richard Parsons.

Text, design, layout and original illustrations © Coordination Group Publications Ltd. (CGP) 2022
All rights reserved.

Photocopying this book is not permitted, even if you have a CLA licence.
Extra copies are available from CGP with next day delivery • 0800 1712 712 • www.cgpbooks.co.uk

Contents

Section 1 – Sentence Punctuation
Capital Letters and Full Stops 4
Question Marks 5
Exclamation Marks 6
Sentence Practice 7

Section 2 – Commas
Commas in Lists 8
Commas to Avoid Confusion 10
Commas After Subordinate Clauses 12
Commas After Fronted Adverbials 14
Commas for Extra Information 16
Comma Practice 18

Section 3 – Brackets and Dashes
Brackets for Extra Information 20
Dashes for Extra Information 22

Section 4 – Apostrophes
Apostrophes for Missing Letters 24
Apostrophes for Single Possession 25
Apostrophes for Plural Possession 26
Its and It's 27
Apostrophe Practice 28

Section 5 – Inverted Commas
Punctuating Speech 30
Punctuating Speech in Two Parts 32

Section 6 – Paragraphs and Layout
Paragraphs 33
Headings and Subheadings 35

Glossary 36
Answers 37

Section 1 — Sentence Punctuation

Capital Letters and Full Stops

Sentences always **start** with a **capital letter** and often finish with a full stop. Sentences with a **full stop** are often **statements** (sentences that **tell** you something). Use **capital letters** for **I** and for **names** of people, places or things.

On Wednesday, I am going to London with my sister.

1) Circle the words below that should have <u>capital letters</u>.

| eiffel tower | castle | tomorrow | spain |
| ashley | city | friday | christmas |

2) Put a <u>tick</u> next to the sentences that use <u>capital letters</u> and <u>full stops</u> correctly and put a <u>cross</u> next to the ones that <u>don't</u>.

mrs Flint is thirty-two her birthday is in may. ☐

My step-mum's favourite sweets can only be bought in Canada. ☐

My Best Friend is called Amy. She lives in Bath ☐

Ellis's dog is called Spot. Spot is a Dalmatian. ☐

I play cricket every Friday evening. ☐

Rewrite the <u>incorrect</u> sentences with capital letters and full stops in the right places.

....

....

 Write a sentence that uses 'I', a sentence that uses a name and a sentence that uses a month. Make sure you use capital letters correctly.

Section 1 — Sentence Punctuation

Question Marks

Questions always end with a question mark and often begin with a question word.

When are we leaving?   Why are you running?

1 Draw lines to match each sentence to the correct punctuation mark.

Where are you going on holiday   Are you feeling OK, Kinga

Here are those gloves you lost   I don't know how to fry an egg

Let's go shopping tomorrow   What's happening out there

Is this your idea of a joke   It's raining a lot this week

Would you like ketchup   We should order pizzas

2 Write a question to match each of the answers given below.

Q: ....

A: I will. I'm excellent at map-reading.

Q: ....

A: A packed lunch and a waterproof jacket.

Use a capital letter to start your sentence, and a question mark at the end.

Q: ....

A: No thanks, I'm a vegetarian.

Q: ....

A: Yes, that's fine. I'll come at six o'clock.

Now Try This — Imagine you are interviewing your favourite celebrity. Write down the first three questions you would ask them.

Section 1 — Sentence Punctuation

Exclamation Marks

Exclamation marks show that something is said loudly or with strong emotion. → That's amazing!

Exclamation marks are also used for strong commands. → Go away!

But if the command isn't urgent or strong, use a full stop. → Pass the salt.

1 Tick the three commands which are most likely to end with an exclamation mark.

Shut up ☐   Quick, get out of here ☐

Let me help you ☐   Please wait here ☐

Stop that, now ☐   Please stop crying ☐

2 Use full stops and exclamation marks to complete these sentences.

Ouch, that really hurt .....

My brother is really good at playing the piano .....

Watch out, it's going to fall over .....

The bathroom is the second door on the left .....

3 Write two sentences using some words from the box and an exclamation mark.

    wonderful   terrible   day   party

....

....

Now Try This — Write a sentence ending with an exclamation mark that you might say if someone gave you an exciting gift.

Sentence Practice

Remember — sentences should always start with a capital letter.
They can end with a full stop, a question mark or an exclamation mark.

1 Write the most likely final punctuation at the end of each sentence. Then write whether each sentence is a question, an exclamation, a command or a statement.

John asked when they were leaving... ➡ ....

How ridiculous those shoes are... ➡ ....

Switch the appliance off at the mains... ➡ ....

What time do you think we should leave... ➡ ....

What an incredible cake that is... ➡ ....

2 Write a sentence for each of the pictures below. Make sure you have one that ends with a full stop, one with a question mark and one with an exclamation mark.

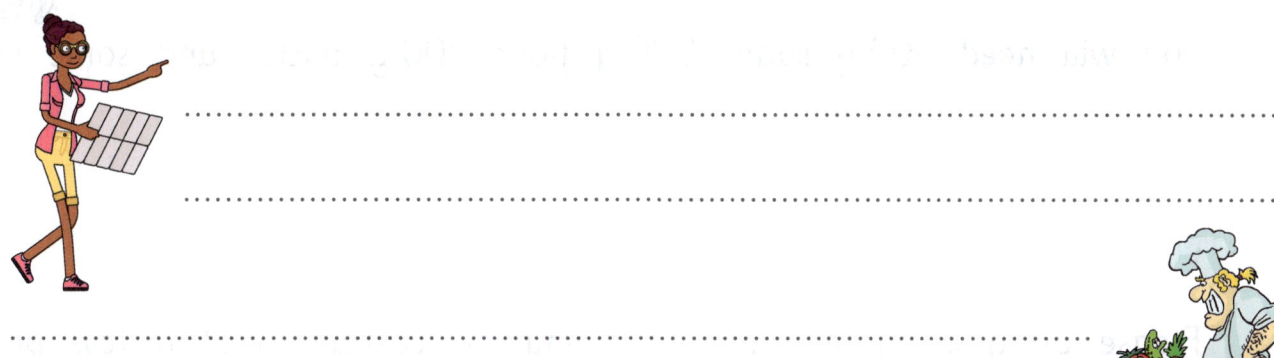

 Write three commands that your teacher might give to your class. Remember to use the correct punctuation.

Section 1 — Sentence Punctuation

Section 2 — Commas

Commas in Lists

Use **commas** to separate **items in a list**. There should be a comma between each thing in a list except the last two. These two are separated with 'and' or 'or'.

> I donated three films, two books, some old clothes and a really difficult puzzle.

1) Add <u>commas</u> in the correct places in this paragraph.

I am going to the supermarket with my mum her sister and my best friend. We need to buy some more cereal a couple of pints of milk a pack of dishcloths and some baking ingredients. We are going to bake some chocolate-chip cookies a batch of flapjacks a sponge cake and a raspberry cheesecake. We haven't got any flour butter sugar or raspberries at the moment.

2) Rewrite these sentences with <u>commas</u> in the correct places.

You will need 500 g sugar 200 g flour 300 g butter and some raisins.

....

....

Please bring a packed lunch a swimming costume and a few pens.

....

....

The journey was quite long very tiring and really boring.

....

....

Section 2 — Commas

③ **Write the items in the list into a sentence using commas in the correct places.**

I need to ....

....

....

....

To do
- clean the kitchen
- bake some flapjacks
- do my homework
- tidy my bedroom

④ **Use the items below to complete the sentences. Each list should have four things in it. Remember to put commas in the correct places.**

a microwave   a brand-new camera   a herd of cows   lots of benches

a squirrel   a week's supply of cake   two theatre tickets   two rabbits

Enter the competition to win ....

....

....

On the walk we saw ....

....

....

Now Try This — Write a sentence that lists at least three things you would take on a trip to the beach. Make sure you put commas in the right places.

Section 2 — Commas

Commas to Avoid Confusion

A sentence might cause confusion if there is more than one possible meaning. Commas help to avoid confusion by making it clearer what a sentence means.

Without commas, this sentence is confusing. → I invited my brothers Sam and Luke.

I invited my brothers, Sam and Luke. ← Adding a comma (or two commas) makes the meaning of the sentence clearer.

I invited my brothers, Sam, and Luke. ←

The sentence with one comma suggests I invited my brothers, who are called Sam and Luke. The sentence with two commas suggests I invited my brothers as well as Sam and Luke.

It's OK to put a comma with 'and' if the sentence is confusing without one.

1) Add a comma to each sentence below to change the meaning.

No babies are cute.

I don't want to fight Jade.

Clara loves painting books and baking cakes.

I only told my parents, James and Aneesah.

2) Read the sentences below. Explain how the meaning of the sentence changes when the comma is added.

I am frightened of cricket bats and thunderstorms.

I am frightened of cricket, bats and thunderstorms.

....
....
....

Section 2 — Commas

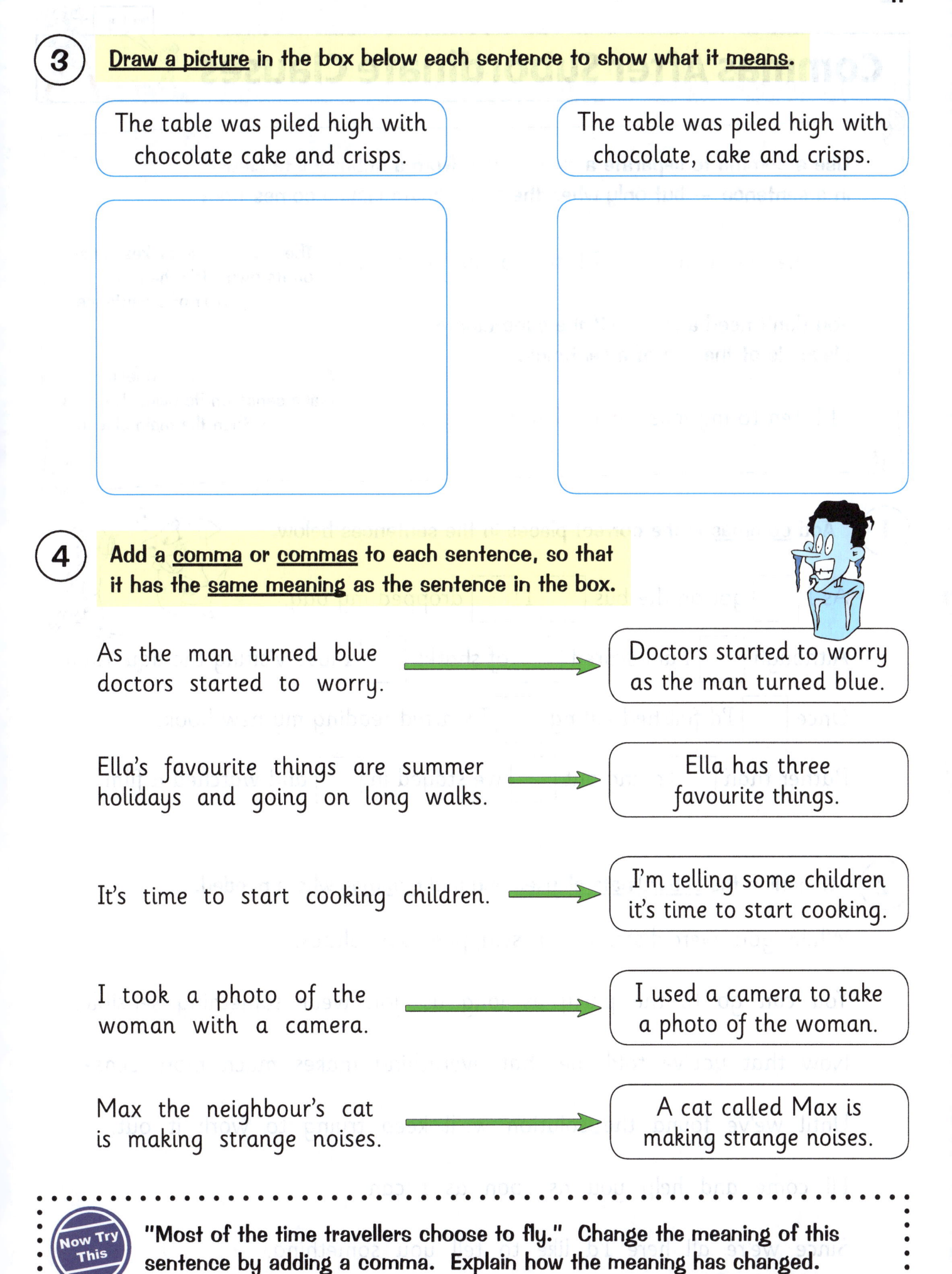

3) <u>Draw a picture</u> in the box below each sentence to show what it <u>means</u>.

The table was piled high with chocolate cake and crisps.	The table was piled high with chocolate, cake and crisps.

4) Add a <u>comma</u> or <u>commas</u> to each sentence, so that it has the <u>same meaning</u> as the sentence in the box.

As the man turned blue doctors started to worry. → Doctors started to worry as the man turned blue.

Ella's favourite things are summer holidays and going on long walks. → Ella has three favourite things.

It's time to start cooking children. → I'm telling some children it's time to start cooking.

I took a photo of the woman with a camera. → I used a camera to take a photo of the woman.

Max the neighbour's cat is making strange noises. → A cat called Max is making strange noises.

Now Try This "Most of the time travellers choose to fly." Change the meaning of this sentence by adding a comma. Explain how the meaning has changed.

Section 2 — Commas

Commas After Subordinate Clauses

Use a comma to separate a main clause from a subordinate clause in a sentence — but only when the subordinate clause comes first.

> While I'm at the gym, I listen to my music.

The main clause makes sense on its own. It's the most important part of a sentence.

You don't need a comma if the subordinate clause is at the end of a sentence.

> I listen to my music while I'm at the gym.

A subordinate clause doesn't make sense on its own. It's less important than the main clause.

1) Add commas in the correct places in the sentences below.

As I ☐ got on the bus ☐ I ☐ dropped my bag.

Although ☐ I am scared ☐ of sharks ☐ I love visiting the aquarium.

Once ☐ I'd finished eating ☐ I started reading my new book.

Rather than ☐ going out ☐ we stayed in ☐ and watched a film.

2) Underline the subordinate clauses and add commas where needed.

While you were distracted I swapped our plates.

You can go to the party as long as you wear something sensible.

Now that you've told me that everything makes much more sense.

Until we've found the solution we'll keep trying to work it out.

I'll come and help you as soon as I can.

Since we're all here I'd like to tell you something.

Section 2 — Commas

3 **Put commas in the sentences that need them.**

I'm really tired because I've been walking all day.

When I realised what I'd done I apologised immediately.

Bob started laughing after we'd told him the joke.

Although I like the album this song isn't my favourite.

As you're older than me you should go first.

4 **Rewrite these sentences with commas in the correct places.**

Even though it was cold I wanted ice cream.

....

Despite the fact we lost we still had fun.

....

Whereas Steffen is calm Nima is always stressed.

....

Before I left the house I turned the lights off.

....

5 **Add a subordinate clause to complete each of these sentences. Remember to use commas correctly.**

.... I need to ring my sister.

.... Raf wasn't offended.

.... Karthik wasn't scared.

Now Try This Write three sentences about what you did last weekend. Each sentence should begin with a subordinate clause. Remember to use commas correctly.

Section 2 — Commas

Commas After Fronted Adverbials

A fronted adverbial is an adverbial phrase at the beginning of a sentence. Fronted adverbials tell you *where*, *when*, *how* or *how often* something happens.
You need a *comma* after a *fronted adverbial*.

On my birthday, we went out for lunch.

1 Add commas in the correct places in the sentences below.

As quietly as possible Adil crept downstairs.

Very quickly Ebele jumped out of bed.

In ten years' time my parents will be sixty.

Earlier today my teacher gave me detention.

In a very silly way Ciaran skipped across the yard.

In the kitchen there's a present for you.

2 Put a tick next to the sentences which use commas correctly and put a cross next to the ones that don't use them correctly.

Before dawn, everything is very peaceful. ☐

In Italy pizza and pasta, are very popular foods. ☐

As quickly as possible, he packed his bags. ☐

Under the new rules, we can't wear jewellery to school. ☐

Last week the boys, won the football match. ☐

Rewrite the incorrect sentences with commas in the right places.

....

....

Section 2 — Commas

3 Rewrite these sentences with commas in the correct places.

Before school Kim made her packed lunch.

....

On Tuesday I am going to the cinema.

....

Every morning my mum runs 5 km.

....

In town there is a really big skate park.

....

4 Match each adverbial phrase to the correct main clause. Then write out the complete sentences. Remember to put commas in the correct places.

Adverbial Phrases	Main clauses
On the left	she crept through the house.
Every year	she set off for school.
Like a mouse	we visit my aunt.
Earlier than usual	you can see my old house.

1. ....

2. ....

3. ....

4. ....

Now Try This Underline the fronted adverbials in question 3. Use them to start four sentences of your own. Make sure you put commas in the correct places.

Section 2 — Commas

Commas for Extra Information

Commas can also be used to separate extra information in a sentence.

They go either side of the extra information.

The pupils, who had eaten lunch, went outside.

The sentence should still make sense when the extra information is removed.

1 Put a tick next to the sentences which use commas correctly and put a cross next to the ones that don't.

The flight, even though it felt really long, only took three hours.

My brothers who are twins, are called Eamon and Archie.

We saw, my teacher Mr Harris, in the park.

Dr Grey, our family doctor, told me to try to get more sleep.

Rewrite the incorrect sentences with commas in the right places.

....

....

....

2 Add commas in the correct places in the sentences below.

On Thursday the day after tomorrow I am going on holiday. I am going with my two sisters Izzy and Amelia and our mum. We're spending a few days in Portugal a really hot country before flying back to England. The holiday which was quite expensive should be really fun.

Section 2 — Commas

3 **Rewrite each sentence with the commas in the correct places.**

The charity auction which raised hundreds of pounds was a great success.

....

....

Pepperoni my favourite pizza topping is a kind of sausage.

....

....

The shepherd who'd lost all his sheep was very upset.

....

....

4 **Rewrite the sentences below, adding the extra information in the boxes. Use commas where they are needed.**

Charles Dickens was born in 1812. (a famous English writer)

....

....

My pet mice are adorable. (called Sammy and Sally)

....

....

My parents get on really well. (who met fifteen years ago)

....

....

Now Try This — Write three sentences. Use commas to add extra information to each one.

Section 2 — Commas

Comma Practice

Use **commas** to make **lists**, avoid **confusion**, after **subordinate clauses**, after **fronted adverbials** and for **extra information**.

Next week, let's play golf.

Ife, my friend, is very tall.

I'm going to draw, Evie.

When I find it, we can go home.

You can have chips, mash or rice.

1 Put a tick next to the sentences that use commas correctly and put a cross next to the sentences that don't.

The Alps, a European mountain range, are popular with skiers. ☐

The bus stops on King Street Russel Lane and Victoria Square. ☐

At the beach, I had an ice cream and read my book. ☐

The book, about electricity looks, quite difficult. ☐

In England the weather, is often grey and cloudy. ☐

Even if, I knew it I wouldn't tell you the answer. ☐

My favourite fruits are apples, oranges, pears and strawberries. ☐

Mrs Williams, our window cleaner, fell off her ladder yesterday. ☐

Rewrite the incorrect sentences with commas in the right places.

....

....

....

....

Section 2 — Commas

2 **Underline the subordinate clauses and add commas where needed.**

Many people came to the fair until it started to rain.

While she was shopping, we prepared her surprise.

Even though I love most fruits, I hate apples.

Remember — a subordinate clause doesn't make sense on its own.

If I get home in time, I'll start making our tea.

Although the pirate was very scary, her parrot was hilarious.

You can help me with the decorations since you're so early.

Provided that you've brought your trunks, we can go swimming today.

You can't go to football practice unless you've done your homework.

3 **Explain how adding or moving a comma changes the meaning of these sentences.**

In the town square, people were looking at the shops.
In the town, square people were looking at the shops.

....

....

....

My least favourite things about school are history teachers and detention.
My least favourite things about school are history, teachers and detention.

....

....

....

 **Write five sentences about your favourite place.
You should use commas for a different reason in each sentence.**

Section 2 — Commas

Section 3 — Brackets and Dashes

Brackets for Extra Information

Brackets are used to **separate extra information** from the rest of a sentence. You always need a **pair** of brackets — never use one on its own.

Uncle Nigel (my dad's older brother) works on a farm.

The bit inside the brackets is the **extra information**. The **rest** of the sentence would still **make sense** without it.

The extra information is sometimes called a parenthesis.

1) Put a <u>tick</u> next to the sentences that use brackets <u>correctly</u>.

Rhinos (an endangered species) mostly live in Africa. ☐

Umaru was late to work yesterday (Tuesday). ☐

The competition was won by Mr Fairclough (a train driver). ☐

Chris was upset (at the result) they should have won. ☐

Abi's dress pink with white flowers (was too long). ☐

Our neighbour (Mrs Bewley) forgot to put the bins out. ☐

2) In each of these sentences there is <u>one</u> bracket in the <u>incorrect</u> position. Cross it out and write a <u>new</u> bracket in the <u>correct</u> position.

Our friends James (and Alun) live across the road.

(When we went fishing last weekend), I caught nothing.

It was too hot (thirty-six degrees for the cat) to go outside.

The majority of us (seventy-five) per cent wanted Fraser to win.

Agata and Akhil our (aunt and uncle) gave us a new sofa.

3 Each of these sentences only has one bracket.
Put the missing one in the correct box.

The portrait (painted ☐ in 1839 ☐ cost Mr Dough a lot of money.

Fatima ☐ finished her knitting ☐ a woolly jumper).

There are eleven players (including a goalkeeper ☐ in a hockey ☐ team.

Logan's tie ☐ black ☐ with sparkly bits) had a hole ☐ in it.

4 Add brackets to the sentences below in the correct positions.

Jenny and Barbara the identical twins work at the same shop .

Arthur Coddle an English author wrote several novels .

The café is closed on Mondays the manager's day off .

'The Rising Sea' my favourite book is about mermaids .

The poodle a breed of dog has lots of fur .

5 Complete each of these sentences by writing your own phrase in the gaps between the brackets.

The main course (..) was delicious.

Hazel's dog (..) likes to chase tennis balls.

The workers (..) didn't turn up for work.

Indira's favourite toy (..) was very old.

Rodney's car (..) pulled up outside.

The supermarket (..) is overrun by mice.

Now Try This Write a simple sentence. Then, rewrite your sentence three times, adding a different piece of extra information in brackets each time.

Section 3 — Brackets and Dashes

Dashes for Extra Information

A pair of dashes can also separate extra information in a sentence.

Mason — the builder — arrived before Nathan.

The dashes go around the extra bit of information.

1 Put a cross next to the sentence which has used dashes incorrectly. Then rewrite this sentence adding dashes correctly.

Gary left his hat — by accident — on top of the car. ☐

We built — a sandcastle a big one — on the beach. ☐

Alex's cat — the one with the stripy tail — eats biscuits. ☐

The girls — especially Sonal and Ailsa — love the sunshine. ☐

....

....

2 Add dashes correctly to the passage below.

Mr Miller the county's finest baker has announced his plans to bake Britain's first gingerbread hotel. The hotel four storeys high will open next summer. Six thousand people many from the local area have applied to stay at the hotel during the first month. Mr Miller's son also a baker will be in charge of the construction of the hotel. Two tonnes of ginger grown specially by Mr Miller will be used in the project. Tim Bury a famous architect thinks that the plan will simply not work.

Section 3 — Brackets and Dashes

3 One of the dashes in each sentence is in the wrong place.
Rewrite each sentence putting it in the right place.

Moussa — and Sonny — the carpenters need some new tools.

....

There is a box of chocolates — a big box in the — kitchen.

....

Adam — forgot his lunch yet again — this morning.

....

Hayley a famous comedian — is performing — tonight.

....

4 Rewrite each of these sentences in the correct order using a pair of dashes.

| my cat | likes to eat tuna | a tabby |

....

| is in the opera | a talented singer | Lea's mum |

....

| a type of ride | the waltzer | makes me dizzy |

....

Now Try This "My sister a doctor is coming to visit at the weekend."
Where should the dashes go in this sentence? How can you tell?

Section 3 — Brackets and Dashes

Section 4 — Apostrophes

Apostrophes for Missing Letters

Use an apostrophe to show where you've left letters out of a shortened word.

you are → you're   might have → might've   will not → won't

Sometimes the shortened word doesn't quite match the words it's made from.

1) Shorten these words using an apostrophe.

she will → ....   they are → ....

they have → ....   where is → ....

who would → ....   that will → ....

he is → ....   must not → ....

2) Write a sentence using shortened versions of the words below.

should   have

....

might   have

....

will   not

....

could   have

....

Now Try This: Write a sentence that uses some words that can be shortened. Then, rewrite the sentence using the shortened versions of those words.

Apostrophes for Single Possession

To show that someone or something owns something, add an apostrophe and 's'. For singular nouns, you always add the 's', even if the word ends in 's' already.

apostrophe + 's'   the cook's pot   the walrus's tusks   apostrophe + 's'

1 Complete these phrases by writing out the word in the box to show possession.

fox → the ...fox's... fur   Jess → .... brother

puppy → our .... bed   kite → the .... tail

bus → the .... seats   pot → the .... lid

2 Add an apostrophe and 's' to these sentences to show possession.

Miss Ellenby class had all got new school bags for the new year. Rosie bag was covered in dinosaurs. Ahmed bag was bright red and had his favourite band faces on it. Robin bag had more pockets than Miss Ellenby said he could ever need!

3 Write a sentence about each picture that uses an apostrophe and an 's' to show possession.

....

....

 Describe what a friend is wearing using apostrophes to show possession.

Section 4 — Apostrophes

Apostrophes for Plural Possession

You can use apostrophes to show possession for plural nouns.

the fairies' castle

the men's room

If a plural noun ends in 's', you only add an apostrophe.

If a plural noun doesn't end in 's', add an apostrophe and an 's'.

1 Cross out the phrases which don't use apostrophes correctly.

belonging to the frogs → ~~the frogs's~~ | the frogs'

belonging to the sisters → the sisters's | the sisters'

belonging to the women → the women's | the womens'

belonging to the birds → the birds's | the birds'

belonging to the mice → the mice's | the mices'

2 Using an apostrophe or an apostrophe and an 's', write down what each group of people or things has.

The flowers have pink petals.   The flowers' petals are pink.

The students have heavy books.   ....

The dice have black spots.   ....

The guitars have metal strings.   ....

The children have blue bricks.   ....

The owls have big eyes.   ....

 "The girls stories were always about her toys adventures." Where should the apostrophes go to show that this sentence is about one girl and two toys?

Section 4 — Apostrophes

Its and It's

The words 'its' and 'it's' mean two different things.

| its | This means 'belonging to it'. → the cat licked its paw |
| it's | This means 'it is' or 'it has'. → it's raining   it's been great |

1 Tick the sentences which use 'its' or 'it's' correctly and cross the sentences that use them incorrectly.

It's fun to travel abroad. ☐   It's my birthday today. ☐

Its got to work this time. ☐   The lion chased its prey. ☐

The panda ate it's dinner. ☐   Its time to go home now. ☐

It's taken no time at all. ☐   The baby threw its toys. ☐

Write out the incorrect sentences using 'its' or 'it's' correctly.

....

....

....

2 Write 'Its' or 'It's' to complete the sentences below.

.... not dark outside yet.   .... sign is falling down.

.... stripes are black and white.   .... the busiest shop in town.

.... park has a jungle gym.   .... home is under the floor.

.... important to eat fruit.   .... got to be finished later.

 "The horse decided to exchange it's purple hat for a green one."
Explain why it is incorrect to use 'it's' in this sentence.

             Section 4 — Apostrophes

Apostrophe Practice

You can use **apostrophes** to show where **letters are missing**, or to show **possession** for nouns. Remember that '**its**' and '**it's**' are two **different words**.

1) Shorten these words using apostrophes.

what will ➡ ....   who is ➡ ....

are not ➡ ....   when has ➡ ....

you would ➡ ....   does not ➡ ....

2) Fill in the missing gaps with the short and long versions of the words.

is not	....		....	let's
....	where'll		....	hasn't
why is	....		we would	....
have not	....		....	he's
....	might've		should not	....

3) Add apostrophes to the underlined words below, if they are needed.

My <u>hamsters</u> name is Hector, and <u>Ive</u> had him for two years.

The shark showed <u>its</u> teeth and swam towards the <u>fishermans</u> boat.

<u>Its</u> been a great day, but now the park is shutting <u>its</u> gates.

<u>Dinas</u> going to her <u>dads</u> house tomorrow because <u>its</u> Wednesday.

Section 4 — Apostrophes

④ **Rewrite** each phrase so that it changes from **singular** to **plural**.

singular		plural
The pig's dirty snout	→	The pigs' dirty snouts
The car's old engine	→	
The woman's red coat	→	
The dress's thin straps	→	
The tiger's sharp claws	→	
The man's good work	→	

⑤ **Draw lines** to **match** each **phrase** to its correct **meaning**.

the girl's cats — one girl owns one cat

the girls' cats — one girl owns two cats

the girl's cat — two girls own one cat

the girls' cat — two girls own two cats

⑥ **Write two sentences** about the **picture**, one using **'its'** and one using **'it's'**.

....

....

Now Try This: Write a short passage about a family member. Make sure your passage uses apostrophes to shorten words and show possession.

Section 4 — Apostrophes

Section 5 — Inverted Commas

Punctuating Speech

Speech always ends with a punctuation mark, which goes inside the speech marks.

If speech starts part-way through the sentence, you need to add a comma before the speech.

Morven said, "Is he ill?"

Speech always starts with a capital letter, even when it isn't at the start of the sentence.

1) Put inverted commas (speech marks) in the correct places in the sentences below.

Fred said happily , This is going to be the best weekend ever .

Rachel , stop that at once ! shouted her aunt .

Please may I buy some sweets to take home ? asked Hannah .

Arundhati said , We need to take a packed lunch with us today .

I want to go and see the tigers first , said Anna excitedly .

2) Circle the punctuation mistake in each sentence, then draw a line to show what the mistake is.

"I don't have any crayons", said Bishan.

"Are you going to the party"? asked Mirek.

Dad shouted, "dinner is ready!"

Emily said "I have a baby brother."

"I'm practising all the time", said Max.

"This cookie is delicious" said Sophie.

My sister asked, "is this your skirt?"

Nasreen shouted "Come here please!"

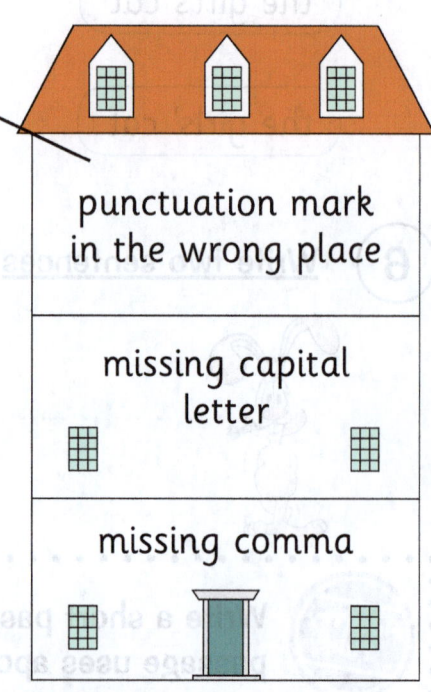

punctuation mark in the wrong place

missing capital letter

missing comma

Section 5 — Inverted Commas

3 Put the correct punctuation marks into the boxes to complete the sentences.

The children shouted [,] "We love Grantham School Hockey Team [!] "

"Today I am going to talk about my hobby [,] " said Nicholas [.]

["] What are we going to do with this monkey [?] " asked Molly.

["] Have you got your passport and your ticket [?] " my aunt asked.

Yasmin yelled [,] "I can see the theme park over there [!] "

"Can we change the channel, please [?] " asked Yusif [.]

4 Rewrite each sentence using inverted commas and the correct punctuation.

I don't feel very well at all said Harry

....

Shufen asked How do I get to the station

....

There's a fire in the gym yelled William

....

5 Use the words below to write a sentence that includes inverted commas.

asked   football   score

....

....

Now Try This — Think of a conversation you recently had with a friend. Write some sentences of speech to show what you both said.

Section 5 — Inverted Commas

Punctuating Speech in Two Parts

Sometimes speech is broken up by other information.

The sentence hasn't finished yet, so you need a comma.

"Look," said Thu, "it's there!"

You still need a comma before the second bit of speech...

You don't need a capital letter if the second bit of speech is part of the same sentence.

...and punctuation at the end.

1) Tick the sentences which are punctuated correctly.

"At long last," said the villain, "the whole world will be mine!" ☐

"That piano over there" said Mr Davidson "needs to be tuned." ☐

"I like apple crumble", said Imogen, "but I prefer blueberry". ☐

"Excuse me," said the lady, "do you know what time it starts?" ☐

2) Put the punctuation in the boxes into each of the sentences. The punctuation is already in the correct order.

" , " , " . " → This drink said Cerys tastes of nothing

" , " , " . " → I think said Rob it's just round here

" , " , " ! " → And then said Sam he just disappeared

3) Rewrite each sentence using inverted commas and the correct punctuation.

I think said Gwen that we should all go

....

Just focus said Nia and it will be fine

....

Now Try This — Rewrite this sentence so that the speech is broken up into two parts:
"That duck is wearing boots and it's juggling," exclaimed Rupa.

Section 5 — Inverted Commas

Section 6 — Paragraphs and Layout

Paragraphs

Paragraphs are used to show when a new subject, place or time is introduced. You also need to start a new paragraph when a new person speaks.

1 Write a sentence that would go in the same paragraph as the sentences below.

Computers are useful for lots of different things. → ....

Last week I went horse riding for the first time. → ....

2 Use paragraph markers (//) to break the following passage into three paragraphs.

On Tuesday, I was playing outside with my friend Mia. She is a great skateboarder. I don't have a skateboard of my own, so I asked Mia if I could have a go on hers. I really wanted to practise. "No," said Mia, "you're not as good as me so you might break it." Last year, Mia got eight chocolate eggs for Easter but she wouldn't let anyone else have any. I don't think Mia is very good at sharing.

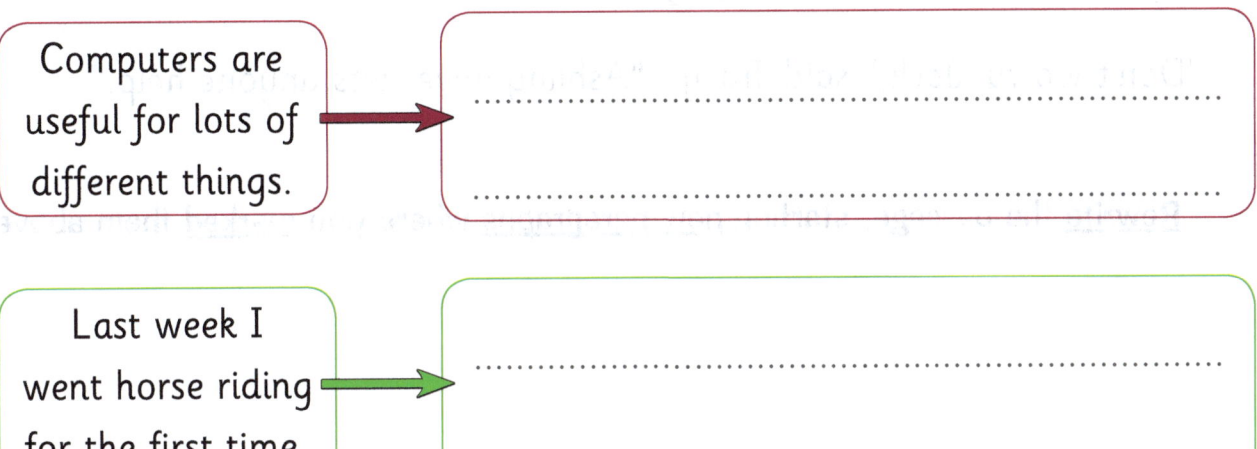

Give a reason for starting each new paragraph.

2nd paragraph ....

3rd paragraph ....

Section 6 — Paragraphs and Layout

3 Put paragraph markers (//) into this passage to show where new paragraphs should start.

"This is hopeless," moaned Ashling, "I can't do it." The maths exercise had taken her most of the lesson already. "It's easy," said Jack. "You're forgetting to add the seven, that's all." Ashling wasn't impressed. She covered the page with her arms and scowled at him. "Don't worry, Jack," said Tracy. "Ashling never lets anyone help."

Rewrite the passage, starting new paragraphs where you marked them above.

....

....

....

....

....

....

....

....

 What are the four reasons why you should start a new paragraph?

Section 6 — Paragraphs and Layout

Headings and Subheadings

Headings and subheadings help with presentation and structure. They are a good way of organising information.

 **1** Draw lines to match the headings to the correct type of text.

- Welcome to Paradise
- A Treat for Your Taste Buds
- More Than Just Books

- A review of a local restaurant
- A leaflet promoting the library
- An advert for a luxury holiday

2 Write a subheading for each of the following paragraphs.

A Happy Future at Tattlefinch High

....

At Tattlefinch High we employ the highest quality teachers across all departments so that your child receives the best education.

....

Our extracurricular programme provides something for every child to enjoy, from trampolining to textiles and cross-country running to cookery.

....

Thanks to a generous grant, we have a brand-new IT room attached to the library and an interactive whiteboard in every single classroom.

 Write a fourth paragraph about Tattlefinch High and give it a subheading.

Section 6 — Paragraphs and Layout

Glossary

COMMON PUNCTUATION MARKS

Apostrophes — show **missing letters** and **possession**. `'`

Brackets — separate **extra information** in a sentence. They can also be called '**parentheses**'. `( )`

Capital letters — used for **starting** sentences and for **names** or **I**. `A`

Commas — used in **lists**, to **join clauses**, to separate **extra information** and after some **introductions**. `,`

Dashes — separate **extra information** in a sentence. `—`

Exclamation marks — show **strong emotions** or **commands**. `!`

Full stops — show where **sentences end**. `.`

Inverted commas — show **direct speech**. `" "`

Question marks — used at the **end** of **questions**. `?`

USEFUL WORDS

Adverbial — A group of words that behaves like an **adverb**.

Conjunction — A word or phrase that **joins** two parts of a sentence, e.g. I play football <u>and</u> I play tennis.

Exclamation — A sentence that shows **strong emotion**, beginning with 'how' or 'what'.

Main clause — A clause that **makes sense** on its own, e.g. <u>I sing in the shower</u> while I wash my hair.

Subordinate clause — A clause that **doesn't make sense** on its own, e.g. I sing in the shower <u>while I wash my hair</u>.

Answers

Section 1 – Sentence Punctuation

Page 4 – Capital Letters and Full Stops

1. You should have circled: eiffel tower, spain, ashley, friday, christmas
2. You should have ticked:
   My step-mum's favourite sweets can only be bought in Canada.
   Ellis's dog is called Spot. Spot is a Dalmatian.
   I play cricket every Friday evening.
   Corrected sentences:
   Mrs Flint is thirty-two. **H**er birthday is in **M**ay.
   My **b**est **f**riend is called Amy. She lives in Bath.

Page 5 – Question Marks

1. Where are you going on holiday**?**
   Here are those gloves you lost**.**
   Let's go shopping tomorrow**.**
   Is this your idea of a joke**?**
   Would you like ketchup**?**
   Are you feeling OK, Kinga**?**
   I don't know how to fry an egg**.**
   What's happening out there**?**
   It's raining a lot this week**.**
   We should order pizzas**.**
2. Any sensible question that begins with a capital letter and ends with a question mark. Examples:
   Who would like to take the map**?**
   What shall I bring with me**?**
   Would you like some chicken**?**
   Can you pick me up from Annie's later**?**

Page 6 – Exclamation Marks

1. You should have ticked:
   Shut up
   Stop that, now
   Quick, get out of here
2. Ouch, that really hurt**!**
   My brother is really good at playing the piano**.**
   Watch out, it's going to fall over**!**
   The bathroom is the second door on the left**.**
3. Any sentences that show strong emotion or something that would be said loudly and end with an exclamation mark. Examples:
   Thanks for inviting me to this wonderful party!
   I've had an absolutely terrible day!

Page 7 – Sentence Practice

1. Jon asked when they were leaving. **(statement)**
   How ridiculous those shoes are! **(exclamation)**
   Switch the appliance off at the mains. **(command)**
   What time do you think we should leave? **(question)**
   What an incredible cake that is! **(exclamation)**
2. Any suitable sentences that use capital letters and punctuation correctly. Example:
   Harriet is on holiday, and she wants to go sightseeing**.**
   Are you ready to be chopped up, little vegetables**?**
   Oh no — my racket is broken and I don't have a spare one**!**

Section 2 – Commas

Pages 8 and 9 – Commas in Lists

1. I am going to the supermarket with my mum, her sister and my best friend. We need to buy some more cereal, a couple of pints of milk, a pack of dishcloths and some baking ingredients. We are going to bake some chocolate-chip cookies, a batch of flapjacks, a sponge cake and a raspberry cheesecake. We haven't got any flour, butter, sugar or raspberries at the moment.
2. You will need 500 g sugar, 200 g flour, 300 g butter and some raisins.
   Please bring a packed lunch, a swimming costume and a few pens.
   The journey was quite long, very tiring and really boring.
3. I need to clean the kitchen, bake some flapjacks, do my homework and tidy my bedroom.
4. Enter the competition to win a microwave, a brand-new camera, a week's supply of cake **or** (OR **and**) two theatre tickets.
   On the walk we saw a herd of cows, lots of benches, a squirrel **and** two rabbits.

Pages 10 and 11 – Commas to Avoid Confusion

1. No, babies are cute.
   I don't want to fight, Jade.
   Clara loves painting, books and baking cakes.
   I only told my parents, James, and Aneesah.
2. Any suitable explanation. Example:
   Without a comma, the sentence means I'm frightened of two things: cricket bats (the sports equipment) and thunderstorms.
   With a comma, the sentence means I'm frightened of three things: cricket (the sport), bats (the animal) and thunderstorms.
3. Any drawings that show two items on the table in the first picture (chocolate-flavoured cake and crisps) and three items on the table in the second picture (chocolate, cake and crisps).
4. As the man turned blue, doctors started to worry.
   Ella's favourite things are summer, holidays and going on long walks.
   It's time to start cooking, children.
   I took a photo of the woman, with a camera.
   Max, the neighbour's cat, is making strange noises.

Pages 12 and 13 – Commas After Subordinate Clauses

1. As I got on the bus, I dropped my bag.
   Although I am scared of sharks, I love visiting the aquarium.
   Once I'd finished eating, I started reading my new book.
   Rather than going out, we stayed in and watched a film.

2. While you were distracted, I swapped our plates.
You can go to the party as long as you wear something sensible.
Now that you've told me that, everything makes much more sense.
Until we've found the solution, we'll keep trying to work it out.
I'll come and help you as soon as I can.
Since we're all here, I'd like to tell you something.

3. The sentences that need commas are:
When I realised what I'd done, I apologised immediately.
Although I like the album, this song isn't my favourite.
As you're older than me, you should go first.

4. Even though it was cold, I wanted ice cream.
Despite the fact we lost, we still had fun.
Whereas Steffen is calm, Nima is always stressed.
Before I left the house, I turned the lights off.

5. Any correct subordinate clause that ends with a comma.
Examples:
After I've eaten, I need to ring my sister.
Despite Ollie's rude comments, Raf wasn't offended.
Even though the film was very frightening, Karthik wasn't scared.

Pages 14 and 15 – Commas After Fronted Adverbials

1. As quietly as possible, Adil crept downstairs.
Very quickly, Ebele jumped out of bed.
In ten years' time, my parents will be sixty.
Earlier today, my teacher gave me detention.
In a very silly way, Ciaran skipped across the yard.
In the kitchen, there's a present for you.

2. You should have ticked:
Before dawn, everything is very peaceful.
As quickly as possible, he packed his bags.
Under the new rules, we can't wear jewellery to school.
Corrected sentences:
In Italy, pizza and pasta are very popular foods.
Last week, the boys won the football match.

3. Before school, Kim made her packed lunch.
On Tuesday, I am going to the cinema.
Every morning, my mum runs 5 km.
In town, there is a really big skate park.

4. On the left, you can see my old house.
Every year, we visit my aunt.
Like a mouse, she crept through the house.
Earlier than usual, she set off for school.

Pages 16 and 17 – Commas for Extra Information

1. You should have ticked:
The flight, even though it felt really long, only took three hours.
Dr Grey, our family doctor, told me to try to get more sleep.
Corrected sentences:
My brothers, who are twins, are called Eamon and Archie.
We saw my teacher, Mr Harris, in the park.

2. On Thursday, the day after tomorrow, I am going on holiday. I am going with my two sisters, Izzy and Amelia, and our mum. We're spending a few days in Portugal, a really hot country, before flying back to England. The holiday, which was quite expensive, should be really fun.

3. The charity auction, which raised hundreds of pounds, was a great success.
Pepperoni, my favourite pizza topping, is a kind of sausage.
The shepherd, who'd lost all his sheep, was very upset.

4. Charles Dickens, a famous English writer, was born in 1812.
My pet mice, called Sammy and Sally, are adorable.
My parents, who met fifteen years ago, get on really well.

Pages 18 and 19 – Comma Practice

1. You should have ticked:
The Alps, a European mountain range, are popular with skiers.
At the beach, I had an ice cream and read my book.
My favourite fruits are apples, oranges, pears and strawberries.
Mrs Williams, our window cleaner, fell off her ladder yesterday.
Corrected sentences:
The bus stops on King Street, Russel Lane and Victoria Square.
The book, about electricity, looks quite difficult.
In England, the weather is often grey and cloudy.
Even if I knew it, I wouldn't tell you the answer.

2. Many people came to the fair until it started to rain.
While she was shopping, we prepared her surprise.
Even though I love most fruits, I hate apples.
If I get home in time, I'll start making our tea.
Although the pirate was very scary, her parrot was hilarious.
You can help me with the decorations since you're so early.
Provided that you've brought your trunks, we can go swimming today.
You can't go to football practice unless you've done your homework.

3. Any suitable explanations. Examples:
The first sentence means that people were looking at the shops in a town square, but the second sentence means that square-shaped people were looking at the shops in a town.
Adding a comma changes the sentence from a list of two things (history teachers and detention) to a list of three things (history, teachers and detention).

Section 3 – Brackets and Dashes

Pages 20 and 21 – Brackets for Extra Information

1. You should have ticked:
Rhinos (an endangered species) mostly live in Africa.
Umaru was late to work yesterday (Tuesday).
The competition was won by Mr Fairclough (a train driver).
Our neighbour (Mrs Bewley) forgot to put the bins out.

2. Our friends (James and Alun) live across the road.
(When we went fishing (last weekend), I caught nothing.
It was too hot (thirty-six degrees) for the cat to go outside.
The majority of us (seventy-five per cent) wanted Fraser to win.
Agata and Akhil (our aunt and uncle) gave us a new sofa.

Answers

3. The portrait (painted in 1839) cost Mr Dough a lot of money.
Fatima finished her knitting (a woolly jumper).
There are eleven players (including a goalkeeper) in a hockey team.
Logan's tie (black with sparkly bits) had a hole in it.

4. Jenny and Barbara (the identical twins) work at the same shop.
Arthur Coddle (an English author) wrote several novels.
The café is closed on Mondays (the manager's day off).
'The Rising Sea' (my favourite book) is about mermaids.
The poodle (a breed of dog) has lots of fur.

5. Any suitable phrases. Examples:
The main course (roast beef) was delicious.
Hazel's dog (a Cocker Spaniel) likes to chase tennis balls.
The workers (who were on strike) didn't turn up for work.
Indira's favourite toy (a rag doll) was very old.
Rodney's car (a yellow three-wheeler) pulled up outside.
The supermarket (the one at the end of the street) is overrun by mice.

Pages 22 and 23 – Dashes for Extra Information

1. You should have crossed this sentence:
We built — a sandcastle a big one — on the beach.
The correct sentence is:
We built a sandcastle — a big one — on the beach.

2. Mr Miller — the county's finest baker — has announced his plans to bake Britain's first gingerbread hotel. The hotel — four storeys high — will open next summer. Six thousand people — many from the local area — have applied to stay at the hotel during the first month. Mr Miller's son — also a baker — will be in charge of the construction of the hotel. Two tonnes of ginger — grown specially by Mr Miller — will be used in the project. Tim Bury — a famous architect — thinks that the plan will simply not work.

3. Moussa and Sonny — the carpenters — need some new tools.
There is a box of chocolates — a big box — in the kitchen.
Adam forgot his lunch — yet again — this morning.
Hayley — a famous comedian — is performing tonight.

4. My cat — a tabby — likes to eat tuna.
Lea's mum — a talented singer — is in the opera.
The waltzer — a type of ride — makes me dizzy.

Section 4 – Apostrophes

Page 24 – Apostrophes for Missing Letters

1. she will — she'll
they have — they've
who would — who'd
he is — he's
they are — they're
where is — where's
that will — that'll
must not — mustn't

2. Any sentence containing the shortened version of each pair of words, with an apostrophe in the correct place.
Examples:
I should've left home earlier this morning.
It might've happened already.
She won't tell anyone your secret.
You could've walked to my house.

Page 25 – Apostrophes for Single Possession

1. puppy's
bus's
Jess's
kite's
pot's

2. You should have added an apostrophe and an 's' to these words:
Ellenby's
Rosie's
Ahmed's
band's
Robin's

3. Any two sentences which use an apostrophe and an 's' to show possession correctly. Examples:
The woman's nails are blue.
The cowboy's trousers are red.

Page 26 – Apostrophes for Plural Possession

1. You should have crossed out these phrases:
the sisters's
the womens'
the birds's
the mices'

2. The students' books are heavy.
The dice's spots are black.
The guitars' strings are metal.
The children's bricks are blue.
The owls' eyes are big.

Page 27 – Its and It's

1. You should have ticked:
It's fun to travel abroad.
It's taken no time at all.
It's my birthday today.
The lion chased its prey.
The baby threw its toys.
Corrected sentences:
It's got to work this time.
The panda ate its dinner.
It's time to go home now.

2. **It's** not dark outside yet.
Its stripes are black and white.
Its park has a jungle gym.
It's important to eat fruit.
Its sign is falling down.
It's the busiest shop in town.
Its home is under the floor.
It's got to be finished later.

Pages 28 and 29 – Apostrophe Practice

1. what will — what'll who is — who's
are not — aren't when has — when's
you would — you'd does not — doesn't

2.

is not	isn't
where will	where'll
why is	why's
have not	haven't
might have	might've

let us	let's
has not	hasn't
we would	we'd
he is (OR) he has	he's
should not	shouldn't

answers

3. You should have added these apostrophes:
   My **hamster's** name is Hector, and **I've** had him for two years.
   The shark showed its teeth and swam towards the **fisherman's** boat.
   It's been a great day, but now the park is shutting its gates.
   Dina's going to her **dad's** house tomorrow because **it's** Wednesday.

4. The cars' old engines
   The women's red coats
   The dresses' thin straps
   The tigers' sharp claws
   The men's good work

5. You should have matched these pairs:
   the girl's cats — one girl owns two cats
   the girls' cats — two girls own two cats
   the girl's cat — one girl owns one cat
   the girls' cat — two girls own one cat

6. Any two sentences where one uses 'its' correctly and the other uses 'it's' correctly. Examples:
   The rabbit is eating its carrot.
   It's a rabbit eating a carrot.

Section 5 – Inverted Commas

Pages 30 and 31 – Punctuating Speech

1. Fred said happily, "This is going to be the best weekend ever."
   "Rachel, stop that at once!" shouted her aunt.
   "Please may I buy some sweets to take home?" asked Hannah.
   Arundhati said, "We need to take a packed lunch with us today."
   "I want to go and see the tigers first," said Anna excitedly.

2. "Are you going to the party"**?** asked Mirek. — punctuation mark in the wrong place
   Dad shouted, "**d**inner is ready!" — missing capital letter
   Emily said**,** "I have a baby brother." — missing comma
   "I'm practising all the time"**,** said Max. — punctuation mark in the wrong place
   "This cookie is delicious**,**" said Sophie. — missing comma
   My sister asked, "**i**s this your skirt?" — missing capital letter
   Nasreen shouted**,** "Come here please!" — missing comma

3. The children shouted, "We love Grantham School Hockey Team**!**"
   "Today I am going to talk about my hobby**,**" said Nicholas**.**
   "What are we going to do with this monkey**?**" asked Molly.
   "Have you got your passport and your ticket**?**" my aunt asked.
   Yasmin yelled, "I can see the theme park over there**!**"
   "Can we change the channel, please**?**" asked Yusif.

4. "I don't feel very well at all**,**" said Harry.
   Shufen asked**,** "How do I get to the station**?**"
   "There's a fire in the gym**!**" yelled William.

5. Any sentence which uses inverted commas correctly with the words in the box. Example:
   "Did you score at football today?" Mum asked.

Page 32 – Punctuating Speech in Two Parts

1. You should have ticked these sentences:
   "At long last," said the villain, "the whole world will be mine!"
   "Excuse me," said the lady, "do you know what time it starts?"

2. "This drink," said Cerys, "tastes of nothing."
   "I think," said Rob, "it's just round here."
   "And then," said Sam, "he just disappeared!"

3. "I think," said Gwen, "that we should all go."
   "Just focus," said Nia, "and it will be fine."

Section 6 – Paragraphs and Layout

Pages 33 and 34 – Paragraphs

1. Any suitable sentences about the same subject.
   Examples:
   You can use them to play computer games.
   It was really scary at first but then I got used to it.

2. You should have added these paragraph markers:
   On Tuesday I was playing outside with my friend Mia. She is a great skateboarder. I don't have a skateboard of my own, so I asked Mia if I could have a go on hers. I really wanted to practise. // "No," said Mia, "you're not as good as me so you might break it." // Last year, Mia got eight chocolate eggs for Easter but she wouldn't let anyone else have any. I don't think Mia is very good at sharing.
   Correct reasons:
   2nd paragraph — new person speaks
   3rd paragraph — new time

3. You should have added these paragraph markers:
   "This is hopeless," moaned Ashling, "I can't do it." The maths exercise had taken her most of the lesson already. // "It's easy," said Jack. "You're forgetting to add the seven, that's all." // Ashling wasn't impressed. She covered the page with her arms and scowled at him. // "Don't worry, Jack" said Tracy. "Ashling never lets anyone help."
   You should have rewritten the passage like this:
      "This is hopeless," moaned Ashling, "I can't do it." The maths exercise had taken her most of the lesson already.
      "It's easy," said Jack. "You're forgetting to add the seven, that's all."
      Ashling wasn't impressed. She covered the page with her arms and scowled at him.
      "Don't worry, Jack," said Tracy. "Ashling never lets anyone help."

Page 35 – Headings and Subheadings

1. You should have matched these pairs:
   Welcome to Paradise — An advert for a luxury holiday
   A Treat for Your Taste Buds — A review of a local restaurant
   More Than Just Books — A leaflet promoting the library

2. Any three subheadings which match the content of the paragraphs.
   Examples:
   The Best Quality Teaching
   After-School Activities for All
   Top of the Range Technology